LIZARDS

Scientific Consultant:
David Dickey
American Museum of Natural History

Photo credits:

Ken Lucas/Visuals Unlimited—Cover; Pages 9, 28-29
Jim Merli/Visuals Unlimited—Cover; Pages 13, 19-21
Tom J. Ulrich/Visuals Unlimited—Cover
J. Alcock/Visuals Unlimited—Cover
Joe McDonald/Visuals Unlimited—Pages 6, 16, 18, 23, 25
Thomas Gula/Visuals Unlimited—Page 7
David L. Pearson/Visuals Unlimited—Page 9
John Gerlach/Visuals Unlimited—Page 15
Gerald & Buff Corsi/Visuals Unlimited—Page 20
Kjell B. Sandved/Visuals Unlimited—Page 25
Nathan W. Cohen/Visuals Unlimited—Page 29
Martin Harvey/Wildlife Collection—Pages 6, 11, 16
Tim Laman/Wildlife Collection—Page 7
Dennis Frieborn/Wildlife Collection—Page 12
Mauricio Handler/Wildlife Collection—Page 14
Jeremy Woodhouse/DRK—Page 8
David Northcott/DRK—Pages 9, 17
Michael Fogden/DRK—Pages 10-11, 21, 26-27
T.A. Wiewandt/DRK—Page 14
M.C. Chamberlain/DRK—Page 15
Stanley Breeden/DRK—Pages 15, 26
John Cancalosi/DRK—Pages 24, 27
Belinda Wright/DRK—Page 26
Joe McDonald/DRK—Page 27
Stephen Dalton/Photo Researchers—Page 20
Zig Leszczynski—End Pages; Pages 6-7, 11-19, 22-26, 28
Breck P. Kent—Pages 7-8, 10, 19, 21-22
Dwight R. Kuhn—Pages 7-8, 12-13, 21
A.B. Sheldon—Pages 19, 23-24
Dan Nedrelo—Page 23

Illustration:
Robin Lee Makowski—Page 18

EYES ON NATURE™

LIZARDS

Written by
Robert Matero

kidsbooks®
Incorporated

LOOK! LIZARDS!

Meet the lizards. Some of these four-legged, scaly creatures can lap up an insect and then disappear before you can even blink. Like snakes, turtles, and crocodiles, lizards are reptiles—distant relatives of the dinosaurs.

SUNBATHERS

Have you ever seen a lizard or any other reptile lying in the sun? These creatures are cold-blooded, and need the sun for warmth. In fact, if a lizard becomes too hot or too cold, its body doesn't work properly.

◄The marine iguana

The sungazer has spiny armor, which it uses for defense.

This Nile monitor lizard has netted a fish.

TOUGH GUY

A lizard's scaly skin is made of keratin, the same material found in your skin, nails, and hair. These tough scales pro-tect the lizard's body from injury.

NO-FAIL TAIL

Most lizards spend their time on land, but some are strong swimmers. Their long, powerful tail helps propel them through the water.

6

◀ Two tokay geckos.

The green tree skink

TAIL OF THE SKINK

Found on every continent except Antarctica, skinks make up a family of over 1,000 different kinds. These lizards are fairly small but have very long tails— usually as long as their body!

The green iguana

IT'S AN IGUANA!

Ranging from southern Canada to almost the tip of South America, iguanas make up the largest lizard family, with over 700 different kinds. They live in many different habitats, such as deserts and rain forests where they feed on plants. These hefty lizards can grow up to six feet long. Some have bizarre features, such as a large flap of skin around their neck, called a *dewlap*.

Male swifts may have patches of brilliant blue and green.

Male agamids are often brightly colored.

IN LIVING COLOR

You may think of lizards as being merely brown or green, but they actually get quite colorful. They can be spotted, speck-led, or multicolored. Some, the chameleons espe-cially, change color, from green to blue or even orange. 9

BODY HEAT

The web-footed gecko basks in the early morning sun. Only when its body has soaked up enough heat will it start hunting.

All reptiles are unable to produce their own body heat the way mammals and birds can. They need the sun's heat to warm their body. Because of their dependence on the sun, most lizards are found in places with warm climates. Many make their home in the desert.

In the desert, the collared lizard hops from rock top to rock top in search of insects and smaller lizards to feed on.

Usually known for their bright colors, chameleons are a different story in the desert. Here, camouflage means blending in with sand and rock.

NO SWEAT

Lizards don't sweat, or lose water through their thick, scaly skin. This ability allows them to live in dry desert climates. But there's a limit to how much heat they can stand. Desert temperatures sometimes reach 120°F. If a desert iguana's temperature rises above 110°F, it could die. To escape this danger, it has to find shade.

A desert iguana

This sand-diving lizard is checking the temperature.

DESERT DIG ▲

To escape the scorching midday sun, some lizards burrow below the surface of the sun-baked sand where the temperatures are cooler.

DANCING FEET ▲

When the sand becomes too hot to walk on, a shovel-snouted lizard begins a strange dance to find relief. First it lifts its two left feet off the burning sand, then its two right feet. For the final step, it lifts all four feet while it rests on its belly.

▼BURROWING GIANTS

Found only on a few small Indonesian islands, the Komodo dragon uses its ten, long, sharp claws to hollow out a burrow in the side of a small hill. Here is where it escapes the hot midday sun, and where it snuggles for warmth when the sun goes down.

11

WHAT'S FOR DINNER?

Most lizards are meat eaters, dining on insects and other prey. Their small, sharp teeth grab and hold their catch while their jaws make a series of quick, snapping movements over the animal. Then they swallow the prey whole.

Having ▶ snared a rodent, this tegu is swallowing its prey.

▲ GREAT SHOT

In less than one second, the chameleon can catch dinner. Its tongue is an amazing hunting weapon. Stretching the combined length of the chameleon's body and tail, the tongue has at its end a sticky pad that picks up insects. Once dinner is attached, the tongue will recoil back inside the mouth.

CACTUS EATERS

Some lizards, such as iguanas and agamids, are vegetarians, preferring to eat plants rather than animals for dinner. It may seem astounding, but iguanas can bite into and eat cactus without so much as an "ouch."

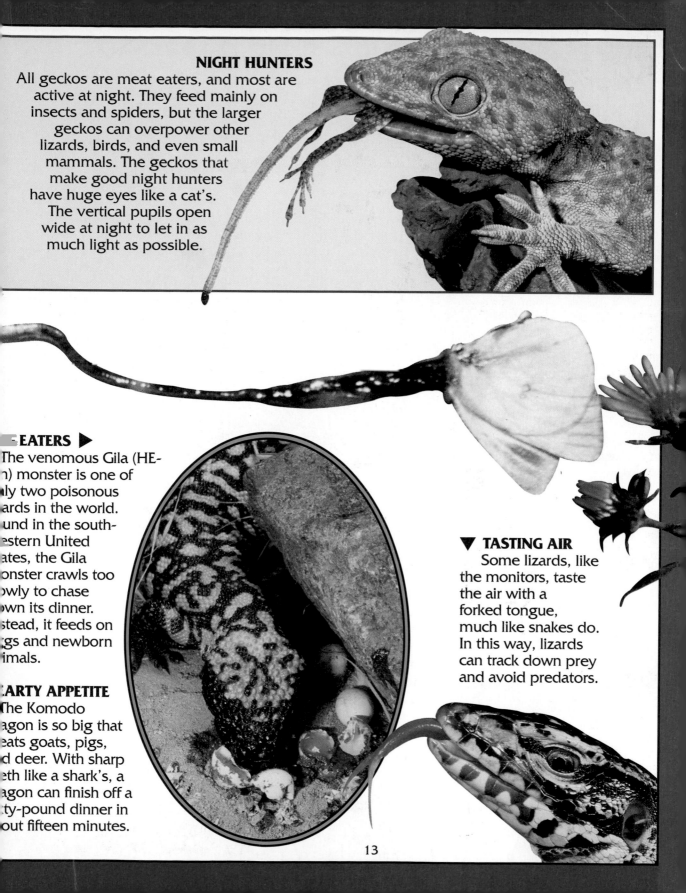

NIGHT HUNTERS

All geckos are meat eaters, and most are active at night. They feed mainly on insects and spiders, but the larger geckos can overpower other lizards, birds, and even small mammals. The geckos that make good night hunters have huge eyes like a cat's. The vertical pupils open wide at night to let in as much light as possible.

◄ EATERS ▶

The venomous Gila (HE-
n) monster is one of
ly two poisonous
ards in the world.
und in the south-
estern United
ates, the Gila
onster crawls too
owly to chase
wn its dinner.
stead, it feeds on
gs and newborn
imals.

ARTY APPETITE

he Komodo
agon is so big that
eats goats, pigs,
d deer. With sharp
eth like a shark's, a
agon can finish off a
ty-pound dinner in
out fifteen minutes.

▼ TASTING AIR

Some lizards, like the monitors, taste the air with a forked tongue, much like snakes do. In this way, lizards can track down prey and avoid predators.

13

GETTING AROUND

Lizards depend on quickness to hunt and keep safe. Most have four legs and use them to move at high speeds. Nature has also given these creatures extra equipment, custom-designed for the places in which they live.

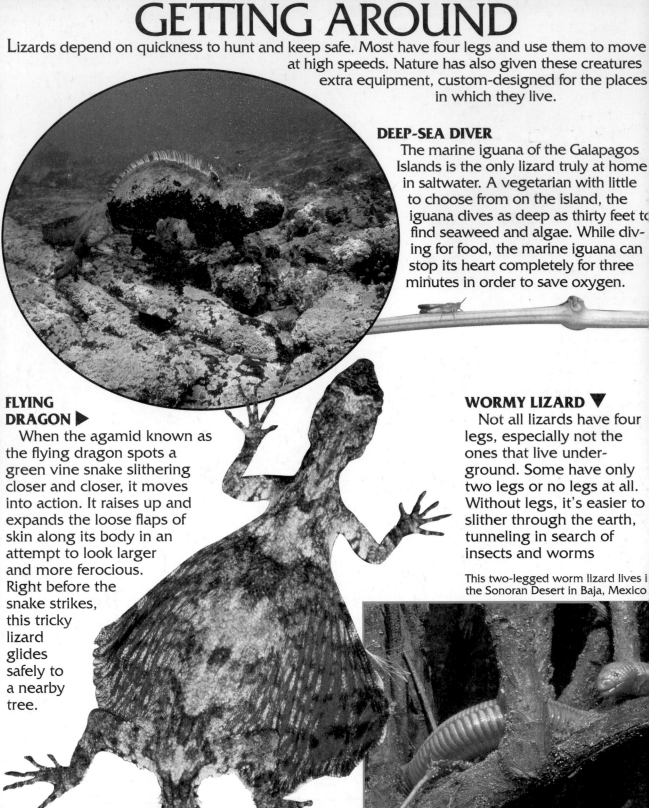

DEEP-SEA DIVER

The marine iguana of the Galapagos Islands is the only lizard truly at home in saltwater. A vegetarian with little to choose from on the island, the iguana dives as deep as thirty feet to find seaweed and algae. While diving for food, the marine iguana can stop its heart completely for three minutes in order to save oxygen.

FLYING DRAGON ▶

When the agamid known as the flying dragon spots a green vine snake slithering closer and closer, it moves into action. It raises up and expands the loose flaps of skin along its body in an attempt to look larger and more ferocious. Right before the snake strikes, this tricky lizard glides safely to a nearby tree.

WORMY LIZARD ▼

Not all lizards have four legs, especially not the ones that live underground. Some have only two legs or no legs at all. Without legs, it's easier to slither through the earth, tunneling in search of insects and worms

This two-legged worm lizard lives i the Sonoran Desert in Baja, Mexico

14

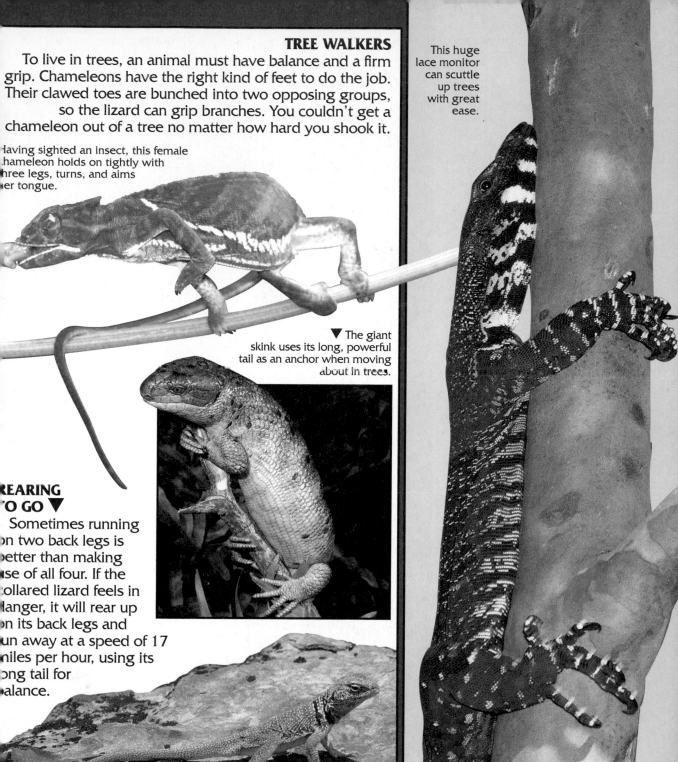

TREE WALKERS

To live in trees, an animal must have balance and a firm grip. Chameleons have the right kind of feet to do the job. Their clawed toes are bunched into two opposing groups, so the lizard can grip branches. You couldn't get a chameleon out of a tree no matter how hard you shook it.

Having sighted an insect, this female chameleon holds on tightly with three legs, turns, and aims her tongue.

This huge lace monitor can scuttle up trees with great ease.

▼ The giant skink uses its long, powerful tail as an anchor when moving about in trees.

REARING TO GO ▼

Sometimes running on two back legs is better than making use of all four. If the collared lizard feels in danger, it will rear up on its back legs and run away at a speed of 17 miles per hour, using its long tail for balance.

KINGS OF COLOR

If you want to see spectacular lizards, look at chameleons. There are about 85 different kinds, and they all have amazing equipment. They have a tongue as long as their body, eyes that can look in two different directions at one time, and a specialized tail and clawed feet that keep them secure in the branches. But chameleons are probably best known for their amazing color changes.

With one eye looking forward and one eye pointed back, this dwarf chameleon looks out for prey and predators.

▲ Here, the carpet chameleon boasts both spots and stripes.

MAGIC PIGMENT

What gives chameleons their color? Tiny particles of material known as pigment, located in the chameleon's skin. Chameleons can be brown, yellow, green, gray, red, or even striped or spotted. It all depends on how and where the pigment moves.

◄ This veiled chameleon is equipped with a helmet-shaped head, sharp claws, and remarkable stripes.

TRUE OR FALSE?

Does a chameleon camouflage itself? No. A chameleon does not "choose" to blend in with its environment. It does not "decide" to change its color. The change happens automatically because of the animal's temperature, the amount of light it's exposed to, or its mood. For example, as a chameleon becomes cooler, it will begin to darken in order to absorb more sunlight.

► As male panther chameleons get ready for battle, they turn bright orange and puff up.

► A panther chameleon hardly blends into its forest background after turning blue.

▼ For this female chameleon, color and pattern communicate a lot. She's telling everyone she's going to have babies.

DECKED OUT ▲

Chameleons are really decorated! They have ornaments such as crests on their back or tail, and flaps and spikes hanging down from their chin. The male Jackson chameleon, shown above, has three horns and a small crested helmet.

17

BABY BOOM

From courtship to birth, baby-making varies from one kind of lizard to another. Usually when courting, males become more brightly colored. But some also do special "dances" to get a female's attention. Most females lay eggs and leave their unhatched babies behind. But some carry the eggs inside their body until they're ready to hatch.

LITTLE IGUANAS

Most mother lizards lay eggs with tough, leathery shells. The green iguana may lay up to 40 at one time. The baby lizards that emerge from the eggs are miniature versions of their parents. Right after they hatch, the babies can find their own food.

WRESTLE MANIA

At the start of each mating season, male Bengal monitor lizards try to impress the ladies with their strength. They wrestle each other for the privilege of mating with a female. It may look like a dance, but it's serious business!

When the ▶ male African rainbow agama wants to get a female's attention, he completes a series of push-ups.

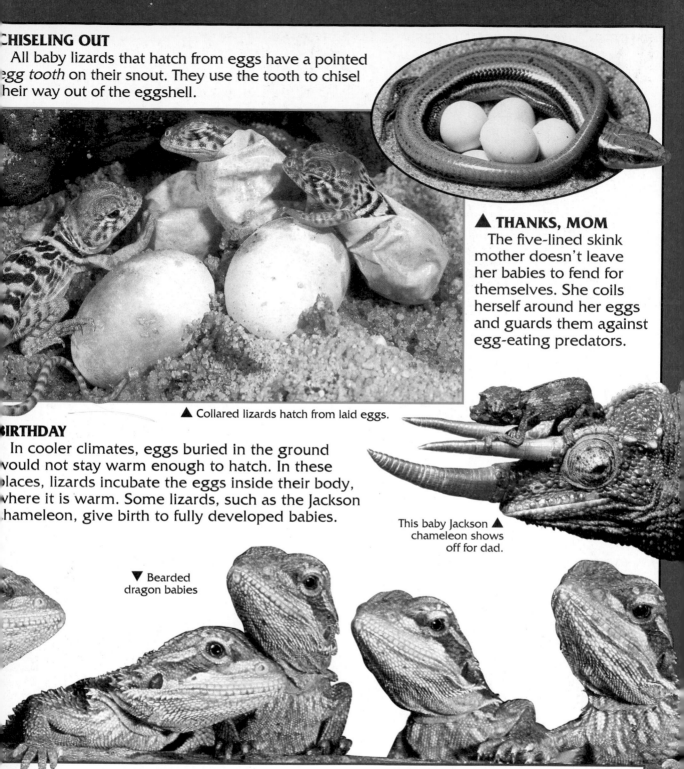

CHISELING OUT

All baby lizards that hatch from eggs have a pointed *egg tooth* on their snout. They use the tooth to chisel their way out of the eggshell.

▲ THANKS, MOM

The five-lined skink mother doesn't leave her babies to fend for themselves. She coils herself around her eggs and guards them against egg-eating predators.

▲ Collared lizards hatch from laid eggs.

BIRTHDAY

In cooler climates, eggs buried in the ground would not stay warm enough to hatch. In these places, lizards incubate the eggs inside their body, where it is warm. Some lizards, such as the Jackson chameleon, give birth to fully developed babies.

This baby Jackson ▲ chameleon shows off for dad.

▼ Bearded dragon babies

SAFETY IN NUMBERS

Lizard babies may start fighting each other very early on, trying to establish a territory. But some babies stick together until they're old enough to take care of themselves. For the first twelve months of life, emerald lizards stay together. When attacked, they scatter in all directions, confusing their attacker and giving themselves a few seconds to escape.

THAT'S AMAZING!

Have you ever seen a lizard with a beard? Do you know there's one lizard that can walk on water? Lizards are amazing. Their antics and armor really set them apart!

◄WALKING ON WATER

The basilisk lizard has an incredible method of escape from its enemies. It rears up on its hind legs and runs across the surface of water. Moving quickly on long, wide toes, the basilisk can take several strides before its body breaks the water's surface and sinks in.

BIG BEARD ►

This lizard does have a beard—a chin full of spiky armor! Known as the bearded dragon, it uses its armor to frighten enemies. It inflates its body, opens its mouth, and expands its big, spiny throat. That's a frightening sight and a big signal to stand clear!

SALT SHAKERS

Marine iguanas are really resourceful when it comes to finding food. They swim the sea looking for seaweed. There's one problem, though. They swallow a large amount of water and get a huge overdose of salt. But their body has developed an amazing trick. It shakes out the salt through special glands in the nasal cavities.

NO-FAIL TAIL

The chameleon is one lizard that can hang by its tail from a branch like a monkey. All lizards have fantastic tails. Some tails are long and are used for balance. Some can be discarded to distract enemies so that the lizard can escape. But only a few are built for strength and allow the lizard to hang out in trees.

THIRST QUENCHER

Getting a drink of water in the desert is not that easy, unless you're a thorny devil. This lizard has sharp spikes covering its body for protection. But the spikes also provide drinking water. Overnight, dew condenses on the thorns, and the water trickles along tiny grooves in the skin to the thorny devil's mouth.

WINDSHIELD WIPER

Most lizards have eyelids, which protect the eyes and help keep them clean. Geckos, however, do not. Instead, they use their long tongue like a windshield wiper, rolling it over their eyes to keep their vision clear!

BYE-BYE SKIN

Lizards never stop growing! Because their skin does not grow with them, they have to shed it. A few use shedding as a defense. Geckos are covered with a very loose layer of skin. The slightest amount of pressure from an attack causes the skin to come off. The lizard escapes, and the attacker is left with an old suit.

21

RUN OR HIDE

Lizards are survivors. One of the reasons they are so successful is that they've developed very effective ways to defend themselves. Most lizards are small creatures who depend on speed and quickness rather than brute strength. Their first line of defense, in fact, is to run or hide.

TIGHT SQUEEZE ▼

While basking in the sun, lizards like to stay close to a rocky crevice or burrow where they can retreat if threatened. But the chuckwalla lizard has an additional defense. When it gets between two rocks, it takes several deep breaths and inflates its body with air. Wedged in tightly, the chuckwalla becomes impossible for an attacker to even budge.

IN THE HOLE ▼

Hiding can be very simple in the desert. A lizard can simply burrow beneath the sand. With only its face showing, this sandy-colored horned lizard could easily be overlooked by a predator.

GOOD PLANNING ▲

A basilisk lizard knows how to take a nap. Living in Brazil's tropical rain forest, it crawls out to the tip of a thin branch that extends out over a small stream. When a hungry snake slithers too close, the branch shakes. With this warning, the basilisk drops into the water, safely out of the snake's reach.

22

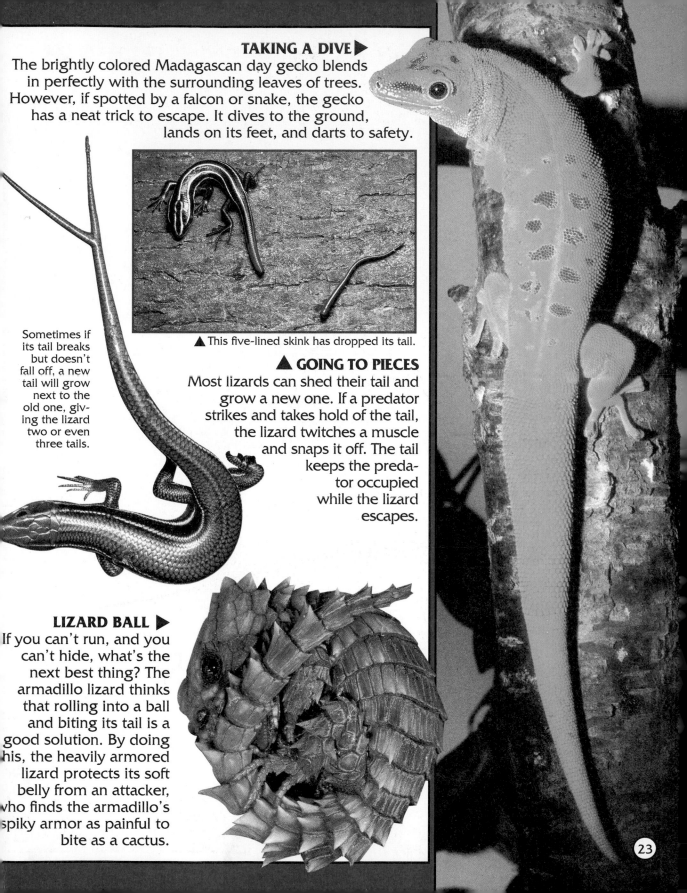

TAKING A DIVE ▶

The brightly colored Madagascan day gecko blends in perfectly with the surrounding leaves of trees. However, if spotted by a falcon or snake, the gecko has a neat trick to escape. It dives to the ground, lands on its feet, and darts to safety.

▲ This five-lined skink has dropped its tail.

▲ GOING TO PIECES

Most lizards can shed their tail and grow a new one. If a predator strikes and takes hold of the tail, the lizard twitches a muscle and snaps it off. The tail keeps the predator occupied while the lizard escapes.

Sometimes if its tail breaks but doesn't fall off, a new tail will grow next to the old one, giving the lizard two or even three tails.

LIZARD BALL ▶

If you can't run, and you can't hide, what's the next best thing? The armadillo lizard thinks that rolling into a ball and biting its tail is a good solution. By doing this, the heavily armored lizard protects its soft belly from an attacker, who finds the armadillo's spiky armor as painful to bite as a cactus.

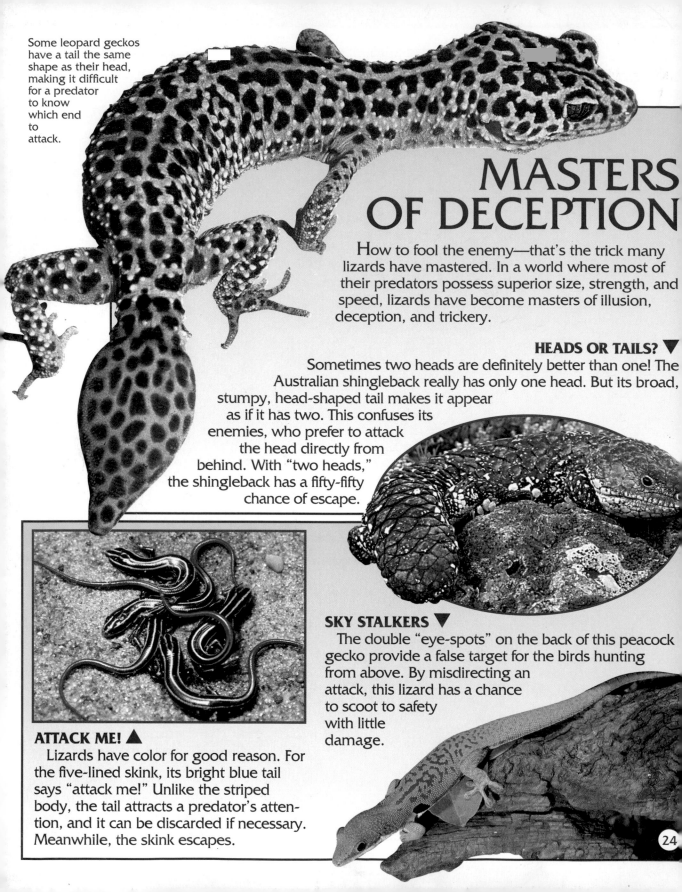

Some leopard geckos have a tail the same shape as their head, making it difficult for a predator to know which end to attack.

MASTERS OF DECEPTION

How to fool the enemy—that's the trick many lizards have mastered. In a world where most of their predators possess superior size, strength, and speed, lizards have become masters of illusion, deception, and trickery.

HEADS OR TAILS? ▼

Sometimes two heads are definitely better than one! The Australian shingleback really has only one head. But its broad, stumpy, head-shaped tail makes it appear as if it has two. This confuses its enemies, who prefer to attack the head directly from behind. With "two heads," the shingleback has a fifty-fifty chance of escape.

SKY STALKERS ▼

The double "eye-spots" on the back of this peacock gecko provide a false target for the birds hunting from above. By misdirecting an attack, this lizard has a chance to scoot to safety with little damage.

ATTACK ME! ▲

Lizards have color for good reason. For the five-lined skink, its bright blue tail says "attack me!" Unlike the striped body, the tail attracts a predator's attention, and it can be discarded if necessary. Meanwhile, the skink escapes.

24

WHERE'S THAT LIZARD?

Camouflage is a nifty little trick. Many lizards are naturally colored to blend in with their habitat, whether it's in the trees of a rain forest, in the desert sand, or on a forest floor.

▲ If you were walking by this tree, would you see this leaf-tailed gecko?

▲ Can you spot a gliding gecko in this photo?

A panther chameleon

FREEZE!

True masters of deception, chameleons know that, when you want to escape a predator, it's sometimes better just to stand still. In the face of danger, chameleons stop and remain motionless. Their color usually blends with their environment, making them doubly hard to spot. An attacker will often go right on by.

PLAYING POSSUM

Some chameleons "play possum," or pretend to be dead. When cornered, the chameleon suddenly drops to the ground on its side, stretches its feet out stiffly, and remains motionless. Most predators prefer a fresh kill to a dead meal, so they sometimes walk away. If not, they at least relax their guard long enough so that the chameleon can run to safety.

25

Standing up on its hind legs, this monitor lizard takes on a threatening posture.

SCARY MOVES

When escape is blocked and a hungry predator is closing in, nature has provided lizards with one last line of defense. A lizard will turn aggressive, trying to scare or intimidate its would-be killer into backing down. If that fails, watch out! The lizard will attack.

▼ STAY AWAY!

If cornered, the Australian frilled lizard rears up on its hind legs, opens its mouth wide, and unfolds the enormous frill around its head. If its attacker is still around, the lizard swings its head to and fro, lashes its long, whiplike tail back and forth, and sounds a long, angry hissss!

POP EYES

A frightened helmeted lizard tries to make himself look as large and ferocious as possible. It raises the bony "helmet" on the back of its skull, inflates the flap of skin around its neck, and bugs out its eyes. After seeing this huge frightening head, many predators realize that they weren't quite as hungry as they thought.

◀ This anole tries to frighten off an intruder by inflating a brightly colored dewlap.

CRYING BLOOD

Horned toads are small lizards with toad-like faces. Their bodies are covered with razor-sharp "horns" or spikes. When cornered, the horny toad will shoot small jets of blood from its eyes. Some people think the blood irritates the eyes of an attacker, but perhaps it just frightens them.

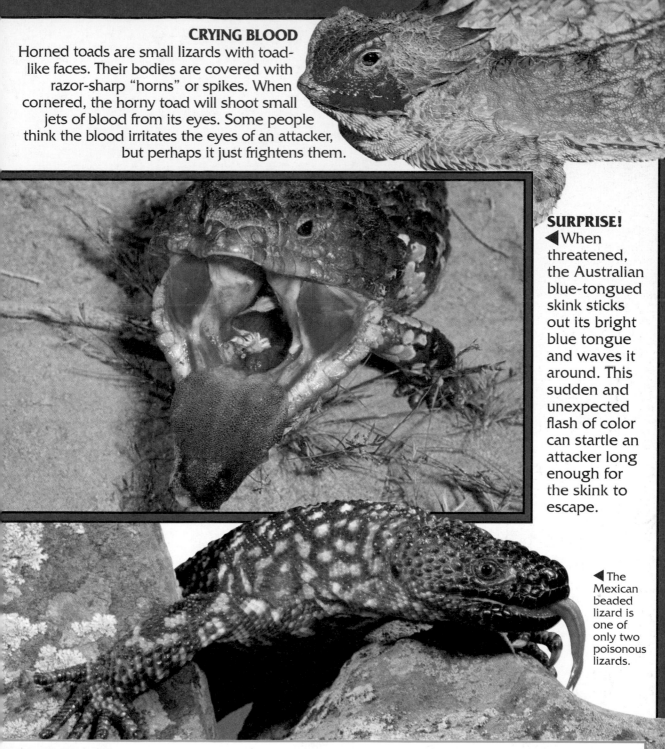

SURPRISE!

◄ When threatened, the Australian blue-tongued skink sticks out its bright blue tongue and waves it around. This sudden and unexpected flash of color can startle an attacker long enough for the skink to escape.

◄ The Mexican beaded lizard is one of only two poisonous lizards.

SLOW DEATH

The Mexican beaded lizard and Gila (Hee-la) monster are poisonous. Once they bite their enemy, they clamp onto it with their teeth. As the lizard struggles to keep its grip, the poison slowly trickles into the wound. The lizard's venom can kill a small animal but rarely kills people.

A LOOK AHEAD

Today a great many lizards are in danger of being killed, due mainly to loss of habitat and hunting. People can help prevent their endangerment. By not purchasing products made from lizards, they can give hunters fewer reasons to kill these incredible creatures.

Dumeril's monitor

Pacific monitor

A TASTY TREAT ▼

Believe it or not, some people find lizards to be tasty treats. In South and Central America iguanas are a delicacy often served to visiting relatives and important guests. However, this custom is not a huge threat to the lizard population

THE PRICE OF BEAUTY ▲

Monitor lizards are beautiful, but they pay a price. Although it is illegal to hunt them, monitors are killed for their skin, which is used to make lizard-skin boots and shoes, pocketbooks, belts, wallets, and briefcases.

POPULAR PETS

For some people, having an exotic pet like a lizard is fashionable. But many lizards die while being captured or transported to pet shops. Of those that survive, a great many die because they are unhappy and unaccustomed to living in captivity.

◄ DEADLY COMPETITION

For years, the Galapagos Island iguana was hunted for sport. Today, something else threatens its existence. Goats, brought onto the island by farmers and ranchers, compete with the Iguana for available but scarce plant life.

DRAGON SLAYERS ▼

Farmers shoot Komodo dragons to protect livestock, but they are not the only dragon slayers. To many people, the Komodo dragon is a frightening creature. Out of this fear and a lack of knowledge, many Komodos have been killed. There are fewer than 1,000 Komodo dragons left. Their endangerment has prompted the Indonesian government to make it illegal to kill them. Now these well known dragons are a treasured tourist attraction.

▲ HABITAT DESTRUCTION

Because the trees in which it lives are being razed, and the land is being cleared for homes, the long-tailed Fijian banded iguana is in serious trouble. Having lost much of its habitat, there is nowhere to hide newly laid eggs, which become easy pickings for the banded iguana's enemy, the mongoose.

29